SCOTLAND'S LAST DAYS OF COLLIERY STEAM

by

Tom Heavyside

This 0-4-0 saddle tank is typical of the products manufactured at the Caledonia Works of Andrew Barclay, Sons & Co. Ltd in Kilmarnock, the main supplier of steam locomotives to the Scottish coal industry. As Works No.1116 it was purchased new in 1910 by the Dalmellington Iron Co. Ltd, the owner of a number of collieries in Ayrshire. With 3ft 8in. diameter wheels, set to a wheelbase of 6ft, the engine was able to negotiate some quite tight curves, while the outside cylinders measured 16in. diameter with a 24in. stroke. The saddle tank held up to 850 gallons of water. The total length over the buffers was 22ft 2¾in. and in full working order it weighed 33 tons. With the boiler pressed to 160lbs per square inch, the locomotive could generate a maximum tractive effort of 18,990lbs when calculated at the usual 85% efficiency. It originally had an open-back cab, but this was enclosed during the mid-1920s to provide a little more protection for the crews. The engine is seen here as NCB No.16 at Barony Colliery, Auchinleck, Ayrshire, in August 1974. At that time the engine had not been repainted for at least ten years as the West Ayr Area was abandoned in January 1964 when the Ayrshire Area was formed; the latter was in turn absorbed into a new Scottish South Area in March 1967. In July 1973 the two Scottish areas, North and South, were combined to create the one Scottish Area.

ACKNOWLEDGEMENTS

My sincere thanks to Paul Abell, Bob Darvill, Chris Gee, Ron Redman, Alan Simpson, Hamish Stevenson, Archie Thom, Don Townsley, and the staff of Wigan Heritage Service for help received in the completion of this volume. Also to the many drivers and shunters who made my visits to various National Coal Board sites during the 1970s so pleasurable by their hospitality and interest.

Many collieries were located amid some pleasant rural surroundings, as for instance Bedlay Colliery at Glenboig, Lanarkshire. Here, an Andrew Barclay 0-4-0ST, Works No.2296 of 1950 (NCB No.17), is seen on 22 May 1974 en route to the BR exchange sidings.

INTRODUCTION

The coal producing areas of Scotland were based mainly within the former county boundaries of Fife, Clackmannan, Stirling, Ayr, Lanark, and the Lothians. Although the properties of coal have been known for centuries, it was not until the development of the steam locomotive, and the consequent expansion of the railway system during the Victorian era, that the mineral was able to be fully exploited by both industrial and domestic users.

While the main line railway companies became the principal carriers of the heavy and bulky black diamonds, often in conjunction with various shipping interests, many coal owners quickly realised the advantages of having their own internal railway systems. Thus, over the years, scores of steam locomotives were purchased to shunt the various collieries and ancillary works, and to transport the output to the nearest staithes or railway exchange sidings.

When the coal industry in the United Kingdom was nationalised on 1 January 1947, in Scotland thirty-one mining companies handed over to the newly-created National Coal Board a total of 170 steam locomotives. All but ten of these were fitted with saddle tanks, 135 with an 0-4-0 wheel arrangement, and there were twenty 0-6-0s and five 0-4-2s. The other ten were 0-6-0 side tanks. While most of these had been produced at the factories of nineteen locomotive builders – and no less than 106 had been constructed by Andrew Barclay, Sons & Co. Ltd of Kilmarnock – among them were a few which had been put together by the colliery owners themselves in their own workshops. These locomotives serviced the needs of precisely 100 collieries and were affectionately referred to by many people as 'pugs'.

During its early years, between 1947 and 1955, the Scottish Division of the NCB took delivery of eighteen new steam locomotives, fifteen being supplied by Andrew Barclay. In addition the stock was augmented by a further seven bought second-hand, the cheque for the last one only being issued in February 1963. However, due to the general decline of the industry, and more efficient methods of working being introduced at some of the larger collieries, the need for locomotives gradually diminished. Furthermore, at some locations steam power was usurped by diesel locomotives, echoing the situation on the general rail network countrywide – the last BR steam locomotives based in Scotland were withdrawn during the spring of 1967.

At the turn of the decade into the 1970s the days of the 'pugs' were obviously numbered, despite the fact that the NCB in Scotland still owned fifty-two steam locomotives (forty of which had originated from the works of Andrew Barclay). They were dispersed between twenty-six sites, including the Central Workshops at Cowdenbeath and at Newbattle, near Edinburgh, although it should be stated that by this time many had already had their fires extinguished for the last time. During the ensuing years their services were dispensed with one by one, and in many ways it was surprising that the last rites were not pronounced in respect of regular daily steam operations until December 1981 when Bedlay Colliery in Glenboig, Lanarkshire, wound its last coal. After this there was just an odd isolated occasion when an engine was steamed, but in the main many were left simply to linger, some for a number of years, in various states of disrepair. However, it is pleasing to report that of the fifty-two engines that survived into the 1970s, thirty-seven have been preserved, albeit scattered far and wide, seven having migrated south across the border into England, while the rest remain in their Scottish homeland. It is indeed fitting that so many of these fine workhorses have been saved for posterity (along with others withdrawn in earlier years), for the steam locomotive gave sterling service to the Scottish coal industry over many decades. Their true value to the coal owners can never be quantified.

As an ardent Lancashire-based steam enthusiast, it was in May 1972 that I enjoyed my first visit to the Scottish coalfields in search of NCB steam. Thereafter I made numerous forays north in order to savour the unmistakable sights, sounds and smells of various steam locomotives hard at work in their everyday environment, simply going about the job for which they were intended. Hopefully the images in this volume will vividly portray the unique atmosphere of those glorious days. It is an era that can never be replicated, but for those of us who were privileged to witness some of it firsthand it will never be erased from our memories.

3

Previous page: Industrial locomotives (as opposed to main line examples) are usually identified by their builder's works number and year of construction. The various manufacturers attached cast plates, usually one on each side of the cab, denoting these details. This is a close-up of the works plate of Andrew Barclay No.2284 of 1949 which was in service at Cairnhill Colliery, Lugar, Ayrshire. The upper Railway Executive registration plate signifies that the engine was authorised to work over certain tracks owned by BR, for example at the exchange sidings, subject to periodic examination.

Happy in their work, the driver and shunter at Comrie Colliery, Saline, Fife, contentedly look out from their cab in May 1974. The smooth and efficient operation of the surface workings, here as elsewhere, depended very much on men such as these. It was critical that they always ensured sufficient empty wagons were available when needed to run under the screens, as well as haul the fully loaded wagons to the BR exchange sidings for onward transportation to the various customers.

A number of former NCB locomotives are now based on the Bo'ness & Kinneil Railway. Looking rather resplendent as NCB East Fife Area No.19, Hunslet-built 'Austerity' 0-6-0ST Works No.3818 of 1954 prepares to depart from under the overall roof at Bo'ness Station with a couple of former Norwegian State Railway coaches on 3 July 1988. The Westinghouse air-braking equipment was fitted at Bo'ness. This is a somewhat different working environment to the days when the engine was allocated to Comrie Colliery, Saline, Fife, during the 1970s (see pages 8 to 13).

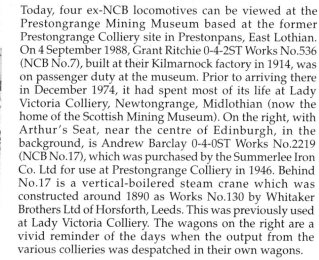

Today, four ex-NCB locomotives can be viewed at the Prestongrange Mining Museum based at the former Prestongrange Colliery site in Prestonpans, East Lothian. On 4 September 1988, Grant Ritchie 0-4-2ST Works No.536 (NCB No.7), built at their Kilmarnock factory in 1914, was on passenger duty at the museum. Prior to arriving there in December 1974, it had spent most of its life at Lady Victoria Colliery, Newtongrange, Midlothian (now the home of the Scottish Mining Museum). On the right, with Arthur's Seat, near the centre of Edinburgh, in the background, is Andrew Barclay 0-4-0ST Works No.2219 (NCB No.17), which was purchased by the Summerlee Iron Co. Ltd for use at Prestongrange Colliery in 1946. Behind No.17 is a vertical-boilered steam crane which was constructed around 1890 as Works No.130 by Whitaker Brothers Ltd of Horsforth, Leeds. This was previously used at Lady Victoria Colliery. The wagons on the right are a vivid reminder of the days when the output from the various collieries was despatched in their own wagons.

The sinking of Manor Powis Colliery, at Causewayhead near Stirling, was commenced by the Manor Powis Coal Co. Ltd in 1910. Until the shafts were abandoned in 1967, it yielded some of the finest anthracite coal in Scotland from the Bannockburn Main seam. Meanwhile, in 1954, a new drift mine, about a mile from the main surface buildings, had been sunk to the less valuable Upper Hirst seam. This coal was hauled by diesel locomotives along a 2ft 6in. gauge railway to the washery, before being forwarded by rail to Kincardine Power Station. Steam remained in charge of the surface railway at the original site until the drift mine was closed in 1972. Andrew Barclay 0-4-0ST Works No.2259, bought new by the NCB in 1949 and numbered 30, is seen here in the rain during its last days at Manor Powis on 12 May 1972. It was subsequently relocated to Frances Colliery, Dysart, Fife. Just out of view to the right stands the famed 220ft high Wallace Monument.

In 1960 the NCB opened a drift mine at Dollar on the southern fringe of the Ochil Hills, at the site of the former Dollar Colliery which had closed six years previously. Coal was drawn from the Upper Hirst seam and transported to Kincardine Power Station by BR along the former North British Railway Devon Valley line. In 1962 380 workers underground, with another sixty-one providing support on the surface, produced 405,925 tons of coal. The mine closed due to various problems, some geological, in June 1973, by which time the only locomotive available for the internal shunting requirements was Andrew Barclay 0-4-0ST Works No.2043 of 1937 (NCB No.6). It is seen here with an open-back cab, sandwiched between a loaded wagon and an empty one, on 11 May 1972. Later, after further service at Kinneil Colliery, Bo'ness, No.6 found sanctuary at the Prestongrange Mining Museum.

Comrie Colliery, Saline, situated in open countryside a few miles south of the Ochil Hills, was regarded as the showpiece colliery in the Fife Coal Company's empire. Work started on the site in July 1935, the shafts eventually reaching a depth of 1,359ft. The first coal was wound in 1940 and by 1947 the annual output was 351,600 tons. In 1962 Comrie employed 1,480 men and the total saleable coal amounted to 425,361 tons. The pit marketed gas, household, industrial and steam coal.

During the early 1970s three Hunslet-designed 'Austerity' 0-6-0STs handled the rail traffic. The first of these engines appeared in 1943, having been ordered by the Ministry of Supply to assist the war effort. They proved to be robust machines, yet easy to maintain, and were so successful, both at home and overseas, that in all 484 were built, the final one appearing in 1964. They had 4ft 3in. diameter wheels, inside cylinders of 18in. x 26in. and turned the scales at 48 tons 5cwt. With a boiler pressure of 170lbs they could exert a tractive effort of 23,870lbs. Over the years Hunslet built 217 of the class themselves at their Jack Lane factory in Leeds, the rest being supplied by six other companies. After the end of the war in 1945 a good number were acquired second-hand by various industrial users, while in 1946 seventy-five were purchased from the MoS by the London & North Eastern Railway and subsequently became the property of BR when the railways were nationalised in 1948. On the main line system they were officially known as the Class J94s.

In these two photographs, taken at Comrie on 22 May 1974, is Works No.3818 (NCB No.19), purchased new from Hunslet by the NCB in 1954. It had previously worked at Michael Colliery, East Wemyss, and at Wellesley Coal Preparation Plant, Methil, both in Fife, before arriving at Comrie in March 1971. On this page the locomotive is drawing a rake of wagons over the weighbridge. The Scottish Rexco Ltd smokeless fuel plant, which opened in January 1964, is to the left.

Comrie supplied the smokeless fuel plant with some of its raw materials. The wooden-bodied wagons were designated for use only between the colliery and the Rexco plant and here they are being shunted from the extensive double-fan of sidings by W.G. Bagnall-built 'Austerity' Works No.2777 of 1945 (NCB No.7) on 11 May 1972. On the left the seven-plank wagon, No.17, is clearly marked 'Rexco'. No.7 was one of fifty-two 'Austerities' constructed by Bagnall's at their Castle Engine Works in Stafford during 1944 and 1945 for the Ministry of Supply. Following its Army career it became in February 1963 the last steam locomotive obtained for use in Scotland by the NCB. That same month it was moved from the War Department Long Marston depot in Warwickshire to Comrie. In 1968 it was fitted with a Giesl ejector, a device patented by Austrian inventor Dr Adolph Giesl-Gieslingen which improved the efficiency of the exhaust blast and as a consequence the overall performance of the locomotive; the distinctive oblong chimney was an integral part of the ejector.

No.19 slowly manoeuvres a long link of wagons under the washer at Comrie on 24 May 1974. To the right of the 'Austerity' is a 2ft 8in. gauge track, used to transport materials around the surface. During the 1970s motive power on the narrow gauge track was provided by three diesel-mechanical locomotives, one built by Hunslet and two by Ruston & Hornsby of Lincoln.

Comrie Colliery was connected to the BR exchange sidings at Oakley, adjacent to the former North British Railway Dunfermline Upper to Alloa route, by a one and a half mile branch line. No.7 is seen here awaiting the signal to proceed across the A907 Dunfermline to Alloa road on 11 May 1972. Note the catch points, just beyond the semaphore signal, protecting the level crossing.

The progress of a learner driver travelling towards Alloa is impeded by No.19 as it storms across the level crossing towards the colliery with empties from Oakley exchange sidings on 22 May 1974. The shunter, whose job it was to operate the signal box, can be seen inside by the large wheel which was used to swing the gates to and fro across the road. He also controlled the traffic signals facing any oncoming vehicles, as well as the semaphores and catch points. This section of railway was originally owned by the North British Railway. Known as the Kinneddar branch, it served Oakley Colliery (closed in the 1930s after being taken over by the Fife Coal Co. in 1924), whose own locomotive worked the traffic to and from the exchange sidings. The Fife Coal Co. purchased the branch from the London & North Eastern Railway (successors to the NBR) in 1937, the line to Comrie veering away to the west of the original alignment, a little way to the north of the level crossing. After utilising diesel locomotives in its last years, Comrie ceased to use rail in 1985 and the colliery itself closed the following year. The land occupied by the pit was subsequently cleared. Fortune looked more favourably on the three 'Austerities' (Giesl ejector-fitted Hunslet Works No.3837 of 1955 (NCB No.5) was the other one), for the trio are now preserved on the Bo'ness & Kinneil Railway.

Opposite: Frances Colliery at Dysart, on the north-eastern outskirts of Kirkcaldy, Fife, occupied an exposed position on the Dubbie Braes on the north bank of the Firth of Forth. Known locally as the 'Dubbie', it was one of three collieries owned by the Earl of Rosslyn's Collieries Ltd, before that company's assets were acquired by the Fife Coal Co. in July 1923. Much of the output came from under the sea; in 1947 the colliery employed 876 men and yielded 265,300 tons of coal. The redevelopment of the pit was completed in 1957 and by 1962 a workforce of 1,322 were responsible for extracting 455,000 tons of coal. The duty locomotive on 24 May 1974, when this and the following photographs at Frances were taken, was Andrew Barclay 0-4-0ST Works No.2259 of 1949 (NCB No.30), transferred from Manor Powis Colliery, Causewayhead, during the spring of 1973. It is seen here shunting the holding sidings at the east end of the layout. The wagon on the right, standing against a backdrop of the Firth of Forth, contained a supply of coal for use by the locomotives.

Right: At rest inside the diminutive brick-based corrugated iron engine shed is Andrew Barclay 0-4-0ST Works No.1142 (NCB No.29). Supplied new to the Fife Coal Co. in 1908, it worked at their Mary Colliery at Lochore until 1950. It arrived at Frances early in 1971 and, in its retirement, can now be seen at the Prestongrange Mining Museum at Prestonpans.

Frances Colliery was linked to the former North British Railway Inverkeithing to Dundee route by a steeply-graded branch half a mile long. Having collected a set of loaded wagons from the holding sidings, the driver of BR Class 20 No.20086 glances at No.30, standing by the weighbridge, as he slowly negotiates the colliery yard while en route back to the main line.

No.30 busies itself in the west yard at Frances. The rail system was rendered redundant in April 1981 (steam working having been concluded a couple of years earlier) when the pit was connected underground to the modern Seafield Colliery, just to the south of Kirkcaldy. Frances closed altogether in 1984, although it was retained for a few years on a care and maintenance basis. Later, when the surface buildings were demolished and the shafts capped, the headgear was left in situ as a poignant reminder of an important aspect of Fife's heritage. Today the site forms an integral part of the highly-scenic Fife Coastal Path. No.30 remains in Fife, albeit as a static exhibit by the preserved concrete headframe of the old Mary Colliery (a former stamping ground of No.29) at the popular 1,000 acre Lochore Meadows Country Park, near Cowdenbeath.

Formerly owned by the Niddrie & Benhar Coal Co. Ltd, the NCB shed at Niddrie, in the eastern suburbs of Edinburgh, at one time looked after the rail interests of four interconnected collieries as well as the nearby brickworks. Two of the collieries, Edmonstone and Niddrie, were closed during the 1920s, while Woolmet and Newcraighall lasted until 1966 and 1968 respectively. With the brickworks also having finished production, the only work that remained for the locomotives in the 1970s was to shunt the adjacent landsale yard and transfer a few wagons to and from the nearby BR exchange sidings, a mission often accomplished in a couple of hours. On 8 May 1972, with the derelict Niddrie fireclay works in the background, Andrew Barclay 0-6-0ST Works No.2358 (NCB No.25), which came new to Niddrie in 1954, runs towards the shed. Notice that the saddle tank does not extend over the smokebox.

On the same day, amid a large volume of accumulated ash outside the shed, the driver checks the sandboxes of No.25. Water was taken from the flexible pipe attached to the shed wall on the left. Business was concluded at the landsale yard at the end of 1972, whereupon No.25 was moved to Polkemmet Colliery at Whitburn, West Lothian.

Kinneil Colliery at Bo'ness (Borrowstounness to give the town its ancient title), on the southern shore of the River Forth, was developed by the NCB between 1951 and 1956 on the site of the old Furnaceyard Colliery which had a history dating back to the 1880s. In 1962 the pit produced 199,301 tons of coal, after topping 200,000 tons in previous years. Then, in 1964, Kinneil was linked underground to Valleyfield Colliery at Newmills, on the opposite bank of the Forth in Fife, and thereafter the mainly high quality reserves of coking coal obtained from under the river by both collieries was brought to the surface for processing at Kinneil. However, from the summer of 1978 the underground conveyors were connected to the Longannet complex of mines on the north side of the river and the flow of coal reversed so that it emerged by Longannet Power Station. This rationalisation signalled the end of the rail system at Kinneil, as indeed also, as far as British Rail were concerned, the remaining three and a half mile section of the former North British Railway branch from Bo'ness Junction, located two miles west of Linlithgow on the Edinburgh to Glasgow Queen Street main line. Passenger services from Bo'ness had been withdrawn back in May 1956. The branch is now operated by the Bo'ness & Kinneil Railway.

In the photographs on this and the next page, taken at Kinneil on 23 May 1974, Andrew Barclay 0-4-0ST Works No.2292 of 1951 (NCB No.21) stands outside the two-road engine shed at the end of the day's shift. As is readily apparent, the 'pug' was kept in immaculate condition by its regular driver, James Spiers. Before arriving at Kinneil in 1971 No.21 had led a somewhat nomadic existence, having previously been employed at the Nellie (Lochgelly), Bowhill (Cardenden) and Rothes (Thornton) collieries, all in Fife, and also at Manor Powis Colliery, Causewayhead, Stirlingshire. Inside the shed at this time was the unusable sister locomotive, Andrew Barclay 0-4-0ST Works No.2157 of 1943 (NCB No.47), which from time to time was robbed of spare parts to help keep No.21 in service. In 1976 Andrew Barclay 0-4-0ST Works No.2043 of 1937 (NCB No.6), previously at Dollar mine (see page 7), arrived at Kinneil via the Cowdenbeath Central Workshops.

The aforementioned 0-4-0STs are all still extant – No.6 is at the Prestongrange Mining Museum at Prestonpans, No.21 is in the care of the Kingdom of Fife Railway Society near Leven, and No.47 is at the Mangapps Farm Railway Museum, Burnham-on-Crouch, Essex. As for Kinneil Colliery itself, the decision was taken to abandon the pit in 1982, while, alas, due to flooding, the Longannet mines were summarily closed in March 2002.

James Spiers looks out from the cab of No.21 at Kinneil Colliery while contemplating his next move. In the best traditions of steam, he was a man who took great pride in his work.

The daily operation of steam locomotives entailed much arduous and dirty work. At the end of the morning shift on 23 May 1974 James Spiers throws out the fire of No.21, prior to running the engine into the shed for the night.

On a grey and dank 12 May 1972, BR Class 20 No.8080 (later renumbered 20080) prepares to haul sixteen loaded wagons away from the colliery yard at Kinneil, while No.21 awaits its next duty. Before No.8080 departed the brake van behind No.21 was attached to the rear of the train.

No.21 ventures onto BR property to give a helping hand to BR Class 20 No.20099 (out of sight at the front of the train), as the two combine forces to lift a heavy load from Kinneil Colliery up the fierce gradient towards Bo'ness Junction. Above the brake van can be seen Longannet Power Station, and a little further along the north bank of the River Forth are the chimneys of Kincardine Power Station. In the background, to the right, are the Ochil Hills.

William Dixon Ltd, one of Scotland's major coal and iron companies, began sinking Polkemmet Colliery at Whitburn, West Lothian, just prior to the outbreak of the First World War, but due to construction work having to be suspended during the war, it was not until 1923 that it became fully operational. The company had invested in Polkemmet principally to supply coal to its own ironworks at Govan, in the Glasgow suburbs, and at Calder, near Airdrie. The pit was noted for its high-grade coking coal and during the mid-1970s was producing over 500,000 tons per annum. Coal from the colliery had to be transported up a steeply-graded 1-in-34 incline a mile in length to the BR exchange sidings on the edge of Polkemmet Moor. The trains were regularly double-headed and here Andrew Barclay 0-6-0ST Works No.885 of 1900 (NCB No.8) pilots the much younger Hunslet 'Austerity' 0-6-0ST Works No.2880 of 1943 (NCB No.17) at the start of the climb to the exchange sidings on 10 May 1972. On the left, in front of the winding gear, empty wagons await their turn to be filled under the screens. No.8 was owned by Dixon's from 1934 and, following the nationalisation of the coal industry in 1947, remained at Polkemmet until December 1977 when it migrated south to the Cambrian Railways Society depot at Oswestry, Shropshire.

Photographed on the same day, but this time with a lighter load of eight wagons, No.17 makes a single-handed assault on the bank. Above the second wagon can be seen the weighbridge over which the empty incoming wagons had to pass as they gravitated towards the screens. The 'Austerity' was purchased by the NCB in 1961 for use at Polkemmet. It is now based on the Bo'ness & Kinneil Railway.

A couple of grimy Andrew Barclay 0-6-0STs provide a stirring spectacle near the exchange sidings on Polkemmet Moor on 23 May 1974. The leading engine is Works No.1175 of 1909, a second NCB No.8 at Polkemmet (this came about due to the earlier rationalisation of the area structure and the engines retaining their old numbers), coupled to Works No.2358 of 1954 (NCB No.25) which had been transferred from Niddrie at the end of 1972. BR accessed the sidings by a short branch from Benhar Junction, situated to the west of Fauldhouse North (now simply Fauldhouse) Station, on the ex-Caledonian Railway Edinburgh to Glasgow Central line. At one time there was also a connection with the former North British Railway Bathgate to Morningside route by Fauldhouse & Crofthead Station.

No.25 again, this time alongside the weighbridge which calculated the gross weight of each wagon as they slowly descended from the screens to the 'fulls' sidings. The net tonnage of saleable coal contained in each wagon was ascertained by deducting the appropriate figures provided by the 'empties' weighbridge. In the background three more Andrew Barclay-built engines can be seen by the various colliery buildings. The one on the right is Works No.1829 of 1924 (NCB No.12), which had been rebuilt in 1970 using the boiler and tanks from Grant Ritchie 0-4-2ST Works No.539 of 1917 (NCB No.15). Steam working at Polkemmet finished in 1980, No.12 eventually being cut-up where it stood in 1987. Previously, in 1981, No.25 had been moved to the Scottish Industrial Railway Centre, near Dalmellington, Ayrshire, for preservation.

Outside the shed on 23 May 1974 the driver adjusts the stopcock to stem the flow of water to the saddle tank of Andrew Barclay Works No.1175 (NCB No.8) after topping it up ready for the next day's work. Note the long-handled shovel propped against the floor of the cab.

On the same day, after a hard morning slogging up the incline to Polkemmet Moor, the driver of No.25 rakes out the ash from the smokebox.

After steam locomotive duties were ended at Polkemmet in 1980, the NCB hired Class 08 diesel locomotives from BR to handle its rail traffic, that is until matters were curtailed by the miners strike of 1984. Production never restarted after the strike. Earlier, in 1979, Andrew Barclay Works No.1175 of 1909 (NCB No.8), suitably spruced up in a new coat of light green paint, lined out in yellow, lettered and numbered appropriately, and carrying the name 'Dardanelles' (the colliery was often referred to by this name as Dixon's were engaged in sinking the shafts at the time of the naval battle there in 1915), was placed on a plinth by the main entrance. When most of the colliery buildings were demolished in 1987 (there are now some industrial units based here), the engine was moved to the nearby Polkemmet Country Park at Whitburn where it remains on display.

In 1954 the NCB opened Cairnhill drift mine at a bleak location near Cronberry, Ayrshire, adjacent to the Anglo–Austral Mines Ltd Gasswater Barytes Mine. In 1955, the first full year of production, the outlet employed seventy-one men and despatched 23,000 tons of industrial coal. By 1957 there were 181 men and the output had increased to 83,000 tons per annum. The one mile branch to the Gasswater exchange sidings, by Cronberry Station on the ex-Glasgow & South Western Railway Muirkirk to Ayr route (from which passenger services were withdrawn on 10 September 1951), was originally owned by Anglo–Austral Mines. In 1960 the NCB took over responsibility for the branch and thereafter also handled the barytes traffic until the Gasswater mine finished production in May 1964. Seen on 21 May 1974 is Andrew Barclay 0-4-0ST Works No.2284 (NCB No.21), which had been reallocated here at the end of 1973, having previously resided at Dunaskin shed on the Waterside system (see pages 37 to 46) since being purchased new by the NCB in 1949. By the mid-1970s rail movements at Cairnhill were rather spasmodic and consequently there was no work for the engine on this particular day. The branch to Cronberry is in the foreground; the rails were lifted in 1978. No.21 is now housed at the Scottish Mining Museum at Newtongrange, while the other locomotive at Cairnhill in 1974, Andrew Barclay 0-4-0ST Works No.2368 of 1955 (NCB No.1) is at the Scottish Industrial Railway Centre near Dalmellington.

The screens at Mauchline Coal Preparation Plant, between Cumnock and Kilmarnock, viewed from the footplate of Andrew Barclay 0-4-0ST Works No.1116 of 1910 (NCB No.16) on 29 August 1973.

Before the assets of the coal industry were vested in the state in January 1947, the colliery at Mauchline (Dykefield) had been operated by Bairds & Dalmellington Ltd. When coal winding ended in 1966 the preparation plant was retained to wash the output from a couple of drift mines established at Lochlea and Sorn in the early 1950s, the coal having to be taken to Mauchline by road. Locomotive duties included shunting the yard and tripping wagons along the one and a quarter mile branch, graded at 1-in-30 in places, to the exchange sidings by the former Glasgow & South Western Railway Glasgow to Carlisle main line. On 30 August 1973 No.16 was observed near the hopper used for landsales – coal can be seen on the elevator which fed the hopper. The plant was closed down in February 1974, No.16 moving later that year to Barony Colliery at Auchinleck, five miles to the south.

Prior to closure in 1989, Barony Colliery at Auchinleck was the last operational deep mine in Ayrshire. It had a chequered history. William Baird & Co. Ltd had instigated work on the site in 1906 and production started in 1912. In 1931 the colliery became part of the Bairds & Dalmellington group and shortly afterwards the new company commenced the sinking of a third shaft as part of a larger redevelopment scheme. The new No.3 shaft eventually reached 2,100ft into the bowels of the earth, making Barony the deepest pit in Scotland at that time. In 1947 the output amounted to 394,000 tons, comprised of gas, household and industrial coal.

Catastrophe struck Barony in 1962 when both the original shafts, first No.2 and then No.1, started to break down, cutting off the ventilation system and leaving the NCB with no alternative other than to lay off over 1,000 employees. Subsequently a new No.4 shaft was constructed and coal production restarted in 1966.

In the photograph on the facing page, taken on 26 August 1974, Andrew Barclay 0-4-0ST Works No.1116 of 1910 (NCB No.16) – seen earlier at Mauchline Coal Preparation Plant in August 1973 – labours away from the colliery along the half mile link to the BR exchange sidings which were situated at the end of a short branch off the ex-Glasgow & South Western Railway Glasgow to Carlisle line. The locomotive is towing a number of modern automatic-discharge merry-go-round wagons and above it can be seen the top of a cooling tower belonging to the South of Scotland Electricity Board's Barony Power Station. Opened in 1957, the generators burned dried colliery slurry, much of it obtained from Barony Colliery. This power station closed in 1982.

On this page Barony's distinctive 180ft high 'A'-frame headgear, with the two pairs of winding wheels set at different levels, towers above Andrew Barclay 0-4-0ST Works No.2369 of 1955 (NCB No.8) on 20 May 1974. Although this was not known at the time of purchase in 1955, No.8 proved to be the last steam locomotive delivered new to the NCB Scottish Division. Today the 'A'-frame remains in position as a gaunt reminder of a once-proud industry, while No.8 is a valued asset on the Derwent Valley Light Railway at Murton, near York.

No.16, seen here with a heavy load in tow on 26 August 1974, had difficulty in surmounting the stiff gradient away from Barony Colliery and Andrew Barclay 0-4-0 diesel-mechanical locomotive Works No.417 of 1957 (NCB No.6) was called upon to render assistance. The duo are pictured at the approach to the BR exchange sidings. No.16 is now domiciled at the Scottish Industrial Railway Centre near Dalmellington, in effect having returned to its original home where it was a member of the Dalmellington Iron Company's fleet from new in 1910, staying there until 1956 when the NCB transferred it to Mauchline Colliery. The diesel was moved to Killoch Colliery at nearby Ochiltree in 1975 and, forty-seven years the junior of No.16, it is perhaps ironic that it was scrapped in 1989.

During the mid-1840s ironmaster Henry Houldsworth founded the Dalmellington Iron Company at Waterside (referred to locally as Dunaskin), three miles north-west of Dalmellington itself, in the remote and windswept Doon Valley in Ayrshire. The location was chosen because of the abundant coal and ironstone deposits in the vicinity. Over the years a number of pits were sunk, both north and south of the ironworks, and an extensive railway network developed. Due to the prevailing economic circumstances at the time the blast furnaces were shut down in 1921 and ten years later, in 1931, the company was taken over by William Baird's, the new combine being incorporated as Bairds & Dalmellington Ltd. In 1947 the seven surviving former DIC pits in the Doon Valley produced a grand total of 480,000 tons of coal, all of which had to be transported to Waterside for processing, and provided employment for 1,480 men. In 1962 the four outlets then connected to the Waterside railway raised 547,844 tons of saleable coal, the combined payroll totalling 1,848. However, by the turn of the decade into the 1970s only the pits at Pennyvenie and Minnivey remained, with the shed being required to steam three engines daily, although for the morning shift only. On 30 August 1973 Andrew Barclay 0-4-0ST Works No.1614 of 1918 (NCB No.19) pushes some wooden-bodied wagons towards the back of Dunaskin Washery (as it was officially known), while to its right fellow AB 0-4-0ST Works No.2284 of 1949 (NCB No.21) stands by. The loaded wagons on the far right are awaiting collection by BR for transportation to Ayr along the former Glasgow & South Western Railway Dalmellington branch, from which passenger services were withdrawn in April 1964.

At the end of the morning shift on 26 August 1974, the driver of Andrew Barclay 0-6-0T Works No.1338 of 1913 (NCB No.17) attends to the locomotive's water requirements, while the fireman is about to check the state of the smokebox. No.17 spent all its working days on the Waterside system, only leaving in 1978 when it was moved to the Central Workshops at Cowdenbeath. In 1980 it was acquired by the Tanfield Railway at Marley Hill, near Gateshead, Tyne & Wear, from the Arniston Withdrawn Machinery Store at Gorebridge, Midlothian. No.17 has 18in. x 24in. outside cylinders and 3ft 9in. diameter wheels with a wheelbase of 6ft 0in. + 5ft 6in. The side tanks hold up to 900 gallons of water and the bunker 35cwt of coal. Length over buffers is 28ft 2¾in. and it tips the scales at 45 tons in full working order. At the maximum working pressure of 160lbs per square inch, tractive effort is 23,500lbs. It is interesting to compare these details with those of Andrew Barclay 0-4-0ST Works No.1116 pictured on page 1.

The duties at Dunaskin regularly took the engines a few miles away from the shed and since they could not carry sufficient fuel for a full day's work, it was the normal practice to couple a wagon, with the front end removed, behind each locomotive, to act as a tender. On 21 May 1974 the fireman replenishes the bunker of Andrew Barclay 0-6-0T Works No.2335 (NCB No.24), built new for the Waterside system in 1953, from six-plank tender-wagon No.E/W/A9 which is clearly marked 'for internal use'. The builder's and Railway Executive's registration plates are attached to the side of the bunker.

The pits at Pennyvenie and Minnivey produced a prodigious amount of waste material which in the 1970s was transported to the tip at Cutler between Dunaskin Washery and Minnivey. Here, No.24 waits on the tip after propelling sixteen side-tipping wagons from Pennyvenie on 27 May 1974. As one of the wagons is being emptied a Caterpillar tractor stands nearby, ready to spread the deposited waste around the site. While No.24 had similar sized cylinders to No.17 (see previous page), other dimensions were slightly larger, and its 3ft 10in. diameter wheels, together with an increased maximum boiler pressure of 180 p.s.i. provided a tractive effort of 25,860lbs, making it even more powerful than its older sister and, indeed, the Hunslet 'Austerities' (see page 9). In full working order it weighed 50 tons 10cwt. However, No.24 was always looked upon as an indifferent steamer, that is until it was fitted with a Giesl ejector in February 1965, whereupon its performance became much improved.

Pennyvenie Colliery on the outskirts of Dalmellington was some three miles to the south-east of Dunaskin Washery. On 21 May 1974 No.24 bides time while some side-tipping wagons are marshalled together, prior to a trip to the Cutler tip.

Coal production from the drift mine at Minnivey, one mile west of Pennyvenie, commenced in 1958. It closed in November 1975. In this view of No.24 at Minnivey on 29 August 1973, the oblong Giesl ejector is seen to advantage, as are the sloping side tanks designed to carry up to 1,185 gallons of water. No.24 has been preserved on the Bo'ness & Kinneil Railway.

Waste was also taken to the Cutler tip from the washery at Dunaskin. With the shunter riding in the tender-wagon, Andrew Barclay 0-4-0ST Works No.2244 of 1947 (NCB No.10) hauls six heavily laden side-tipping wagons towards the tip on the rather murky morning of 27 May 1974. In the spring of 1976 No.10 was moved the short distance to Killoch Colliery at Ochiltree (opened in 1960), as cover for some temperamental diesels. It returned to Waterside at the end of 1977.

No.19 has just passed Minnivey mine (which can be seen on the right) while en route to Dunaskin Washery with a lengthy haul of coal hewn at Pennyvenie on 29 August 1973. At the far end of the loop, No.24, pulling a set of wooden-bodied wagons, continues its journey in the opposite direction.

Above: A once familiar sight to be had from the A713 Ayr to Castle Douglas road. On the same day as the previous picture, No.19 ambles through the countryside with a rake of empty wagons destined for Pennyvenie Colliery.

Below: The driver of No.10 takes a breather as four of his workmates prepare to unload the contents of the third wagon from the left on to the tip at Cutler on 27 May 1974.

The desolate terrain in this part of the Doon Valley is evident in this photograph of No.24 making its way towards Dunaskin with coal from Pennyvenie on 21 May 1974.

Back at Dunaskin Washery, No.10 is seen shunting on 26 August 1974. Production finished at Pennyvenie Colliery in July 1978, bringing an end to steam working, although the washery remained open for a number of years as the Benbain Disposal Point under the auspices of the NCB Opencast Executive. Currently, the former NCB-owned engine shed at Dunaskin, together with the Minnivey site, provide a dual base for the Scottish Industrial Railway Centre which has custody of no less than nine Andrew Barclay-built steam locomotives. Among them are four – NCB Nos.1 (AB 2368 of 1955), 10 (AB 2244 of 1947), 16 (AB 1116 of 1910) and 19 (AB 1614 of 1918) – which operated over the Waterside system at some stage in their careers; in fact No.19 never worked anywhere else.

Situated amid some pleasant farmland three miles north of Coatbridge, Bedlay Colliery at Glenboig, Lanarkshire, had the dubious distinction of being the last colliery in Scotland to operate steam locomotives in normal everyday service. William Baird & Co. Ltd first began work on the site in 1902 with a view to tapping the very good quality, although rather thin, seams of coking coal in the area. Coal extraction by means of the two shafts, sunk to a maximum depth of 1,232ft, had begun by 1905 and two years later Baird's commenced the construction of sixty Semet–Solvay coke ovens on land adjacent to the colliery, although these were abandoned in 1941. Earlier, a new No.3 shaft had been added in 1926. In 1947, under the ownership of the NCB, the pit lifted 160,000 tons of coal and employed 460 men underground and 111 on the surface. Some redevelopment work was undertaken during the mid-1950s and in 1962 the output had increased to 228,000 tons from a total workforce of 928.

As far as railway enthusiasts were concerned, during the 1970s the star attraction at Bedlay was undoubtedly the Hudswell Clarke-built 0-6-0T Works No.895. The engine had originally been supplied by the Leeds based company in 1909 to the Wemyss Coal Co. Ltd in Fife for use at their various collieries and associated railway, and thereafter remained on the Fife Coast until it arrived at Bedlay in 1968. It was equipped with inside cylinders measuring 17½in. x 26in. and 4ft 2in. diameter wheels. The side tanks extended from the cab to the front of the smokebox and it weighed 46 tons 7cwt in working order. At the maximum boiler pressure of 160lbs tractive effort was 21,660lbs. Throughout its life, both in its Wemyss Coal Co. and NCB days, it was allocated running number 9.

In this tranquil scene at Bedlay on 15 May 1978, No.9 is slowly reversing a long string of empties over the weighbridge – the weighbridge hut can just be seen above the cab of the locomotive. The colliery itself is out of sight to the left, by the large mound of bing (colliery waste) in the background.

A panorama of Bedlay Colliery, looking from the south on 15 May 1978 as No.9 propels empty wagons towards the back of the colliery. Stabled on the locomotive holding siding (no shed was provided at Bedlay), just to the right of No.9, is Andrew Barclay 0-4-0ST Works No.2296 of 1950 (NCB No.17), whose wheels first touched Bedlay metals in June 1973.

On the same day as the previous two pictures, No.9 darkens the sky as it heads along the three-quarter mile branch to the BR exchange sidings at Leckethill with a load of coking coal destined for the British Steel Corporation Ravenscraig Works at Motherwell. A connection was made at Leckethill with what had once been the tracks of the historic Monkland & Kirkintilloch Railway, although by 1905 (when Bedlay started production) the line was under the control of the North British Railway. Currently No.9 is an exhibit at the Summerlee Heritage Park in Coatbridge.